To My Cousins Evelyn + Jack
It's great to be part of
your family. Enjoy!
Gladys

11/23/10

A JOURNEY IN STONE
AND WOOD

Curator
Lisa Scandaliato

Photographer
Pauline Shapiro

Designer
Ana Martínez

Printing
Editorial MIC, Spain

Library of Congress Cataloging-in-Publication Data

Roth, Gladys Thompson.
A journey in stone and wood / essay by Gladys Thompson Roth.
p. 98   cm. 23 x 24

Published to accompany an exhibition held at
the QCC Art Gallery, the City University of New York,
Bayside, N.Y., Dec. 2, 2010-Feb. 30, 2011.

ISBN 978-0-9799382-6-9 (alk. paper)

1. Roth, Gladys Thompson--Exhibitions.
 I. QCC Art Gallery. II. Title.

NB237.R7765A4 2010
730.92--dc22
                            2010039021

A JOURNEY IN STONE AND WOOD

GLADYS THOMPSON ROTH

QCC ART GALLERY
The City University of New York

INTRODUCTION

*W*ITHIN THE REALM OF THE NATURAL MATERIALS, a Gladys Thompson-Roth uses in her work both figurative and abstract forms and is able to express with subtle sensual qualities to bring us to a meditative state. Exploring both human forms and relationships. Her works are visible proof of her ability to express her own reality within today's society, values that today seem difficult to define and embrace. It may sound like a cliché, yet her reality is projected in such pieces as *My Mother/Myself, Sharing Wisdom* and *Caring*. Whether or not her pieces are just waiting to come alive, they leave us with the perception of human virtues close to be or totally forgotten.

"Art is a solitary vocation." I forget the origin of this thought, but without question it is what Gladys faces within this realm of silence. These personal creative events are perched between confrontations facing her and the actual culture and social-historical bounds that constrain her. Yet it can come into its own only by entering into a dialog with nature, which totally surrounds her existential world.

Ms. Thompson-Roth's expressions immortalize basic biomorphic and organic forms, but fall within the power of reality. The restorative and reciprocal nurturing which surround the spaces are characteristics inspired by the sculptors of our time. She masterly transformed all materials in her exploration, creating an illumination that evokes an awakening to embrace truth and beauty.

Faustino Quintanilla
QCC ART GALLERY
EXECUTIVE DIRECTOR

FORWARD

WHAT FOLLOWS ARE REFLECTIONS on connectedness/separateness and the moral core and fiber that inhabit this condition of being separate and being-in-relation to another, a theme I encounter everywhere in Gladys Thompson Roth's figurative and abstract sculptures.

Reciprocal caring; maternal nurturing; commitment to sharing and preserving the wisdom of our species; respecting, affirming and validating deeply rooted ties of kinship that nourish and mark our identities as individual human beings, separate and in connection with one another – these values – the values in the matter inhabit Roth's sculptures in stone, clay, and wood.

For me, the extraordinary power of this collection, and its urgent pertinence, I would add, are strongly linked to the particular qualities of the sculptor/s creativity --including her ability to discern, name, materialize and symbolize, in and through these lovingly and masterfully sculpted forms, the values— ethical precepts and imperative that deeply structure our connections/separateness and constitute its moral center and fiber.

Could it be that part of the artist's message to her viewers takes the form of an invitation and challenge to participate in the work of creating that fragile center and making it hold, as though the stakes had never been higher -- as though, should the center fail to hold, as the poet warns, the inevitable outcome will be dissolution, chaos?

Darline Levy,
ASSOCIATE PROFESSOR OF HISTORY EMERITUS,
NEW YORK UNIVERSITY

A JOURNEY IN *S*TONE *A*ND WOOD

*M*Y WORK IS INSPIRED BY HUMAN FORMS AND RELATIONSHIPS. Direct carving in stone and wood convey the vitality of my subjects. The materials become alive and elicit the great variety in which they assert their character.

Over 35 years ago I joined a class in clay modeling in a community in Westchester called Lake Mohegan. We used live models who were friends and neighbors. The process of building with clay produced two heads, *Allen* and *Carol* (1985).

In 1989, I met Aline Geist who studied with Alfred Van Loen. Aline introduced me to direct carving. Her background in music and dance transmitted the concept of movement and rhythm to sculpture.

One of the first pieces I carved was *Unfurled* (1988) from a piece of coca – bola wood from Brazil. It was so "alive" and I was so allergic to it that I sneezed my way through the entire piece.

With Aline I concentrated on expressing feelings. I exhibited a piece in a show called *Caring* (1987). It is an abstract alabaster piece depicting two half-circles entwined. I gave it to a friend who was chronically ill. Since I have difficulty parting with my work, I had it cast in bronze. When my friend died, the family returned the original piece and I now own both.

Three other teachers influenced my work: Elsie Nydorf, Raymond Rocklin and Lissy Dennett. I continued to explore the use and care of tools as well as learning to appreciate the various woods and stones. Lissy Dennett particularly emphasized polishing stones, helping me develop many techniques. There were times I left a piece unpolished, believing the rough texture suited the subject and stone better. However, using the same stone for *Shona* (2002) I chose to give it a high shine producing an effect like ebony. It was inspired by the work of the African tribe, Shona. In 2008, it won "Best in Show' award in an Artist's Network exhibition.

Stones like alabaster, marble, African wonderstone, onyx, soapstone and limestone are all part of my repertoire. I used Carrara marble to create a piece called *Homage to Arp.* The stone is pure white and called for an abstract form. Because marble is so hard, it is difficult to carve by hand. I never did another marble piece. Instead, I used alabaster of all kinds.

For the most part I prefer stones with little or no color or grain so that they don't detract from the design. *Flowerbird* (1991) is one such piece. In that piece I carved the petals (wings) as thin as I could without breaking through so that they are almost transparent. *Lady with Hair* (1986) is another pure white piece.

Woods like coca-bola, walnut, Honduras mahogany, lignum vitae, and tulipwood each have different textures and density. Lignum vitae is the most challenging because it is basically very hard and has two shades of wood (beige and brown) inherent in the grain. Working around these gradations provided the inspiration for *Tropical Birds* (2001) and *My Mother, Myself* (2007).

I acquired some discarded wood from the Steinway Piano Workshop (walnut, mahogany). Other pieces come from local trees (tulip, maple) cut down to make room for new houses.

Finding a form within a block of stone or a piece of wood is an adventure. Materials react differently to the tools. The sounds of stone responding to a chisel are part of the music and rhythm of carving. Wood is more temperamental than stone. It splinters when carved against the grain. Working with Lignum vitae is still another experience. Parts of it are so dense and hard that it is used for ships and mallets.

The flaws in some woods like splits and knots were included and incorporated into the design of *Young Girl* (walnut, 2002) and *Tangled Vines* (Tulipwood, 2003). *Tangled Vines* was inspired by a collection of poems about mothers and daughters. I used a piece of tulipwood from a tree felled in my garden.

Onyx cracks easily and one large piece turned into two pieces when it broke in half *Polar Birds* (Onyx, 1996). This is the only piece that has sharp, angular lines, I prefer soft, round forms.

My bachelor's degree in Early Childhood Education from Brooklyn College and a master's degree in Special Education from New York University deepened my connection to women and children as well as the roles of teacher, wife, mother, and daughter which influenced my choice of subjects.

For the last thirty years, I have been involved in the Women's Movement as a Director of Womanspace, a women-centered organization. It has informed my work by focusing on the beauty and strengths of womankind: *Free to Be Me* (1992), *Bonding* (1990), *Pregnant Woman* (1994), *A Women's Back* (2005), *Hatshepsut* (1995), and *Woman* (1999).

Hatshepsut was created after a trip to Egypt where I was so impressed with the woman/Pharaoh who did so much to improve the lives of her people by maintaining peace and creating beautiful temples. She reigned from 1476 - 1468 BC and managed to rule by relegating her husband and regent to the background.

Fagy (1990), a mahogany piece, was completed after my friend Fagy died. It is symbolic of her young naïve approach to life.

The two fat dancers (alabaster, 2006) were inspired by Botero, whose satiric, humorous works I admire.

Gladys Thompson Roth

A JOURNEY IN A STONE AND WOOD:

Fifteen Questions for Gladys Thompson Roth

Alison de Lima Greene
CURATOR
CONTEMPORARY ART & SPECIAL PROJECTS
THE MUSEUM OF FINE ARTS, HOUSTON

1. **I always like to start my conversation with artist by asking the simple questions. What led you fist to sculpture?**

My work is inspired by human forms and relationships, I had experimented with drawing and painting, watercolors and oils- starting clay sculpture was somewhat accidental.

2. **I know that some of your earliest sculptures were executed in clay. Where did you first learn your craft? Did you work from live models?**

Over thirty-five years ago I joined a class in clay modeling in a community in Westchester call Lake Mohegan. We worked with live models, most of whom were friends and neighbors. I was not happy with most of what I did and threw them out. Only two heads are left, Allen, and Carol.

3. **You bring an incredible level of refinement to woodcarving and stone cutting. Was there a particular teacher or mentor who was particularly important to you?**

I learned direct carving in 1987 from Aline Geist, who studied with Alfred van Loen. Her background in music and dance transmitted the concept of movement and rhythm to sculpture. From Aline I learned to see three-dimensional forms and the techniques to execute them in stone and wood.

Direct carving in stone and wood conveys the vitality of my subjects. The materials become alive and elicit the great variety in which they assert their character. One of the first pieces I carved was *Unfurled, 1988*. It was made from a piece of coca-bola wood from Brazil. It was so "alive" and I was so allergic to it that I sneezed my way through the entire piece!

Three other teaches influenced my work: Elsie Nydorf, Raymond Rocklin, and Lissy Dennett. I continued to explore the use and care of tools, as well as to appreciate the carious woods and stones. Lissy Dennet particularly emphasized polishing stones, helping me develop and refine many techniques. However, there were times when I left a piece unpolished, believing the rough texture suited the subject and stone more appropriately, such as *Women, 1999*, which I made from African wonderstone.

4. **One of the earliest sculpture gathered here is the 1986 alabaster *Head*. Do you consider this an important beginning or turning point in your work?**

Actually, a piece title *Caring, 1987*, marks what I would call a turning point-it. Is an abstract alabaster piece depicting two half circles entwined. Though Aline's guidance I was learning to express feeling through form.

Caring also has a special history on another level. I gave it to a friend who was chronically ill. Since I have difficulty parting with my work, I had it cast in bronze. When my friend died, the family returned the original piece, so now the two versions are united.

5. **Although you rarely (if ever) apply color to your figures, your work explores an amazing range of tonalities. Do you find inspiration in white or rose tones of alabaster? Or warm grain of certain woods?**

Stones line alabaster, marble, African wonderstone, onyx, soapstone and limestone are all part of my repertoire. I used Carrara marble to create a piece called

Homage to Arp. The stone is pure white and called for an abstract form.

For the most part, I prefer stones with little or no color or grain so that they don't detract from the design. *Flowerbird, 1991,* is once such piece. I carved the white petals (or wings) as thinly as I could without breaking through, so that they are almost transparent. *Lady with Hair, 1986,*is another pure white piece.

Woods like coca-bola, walnut, Honduras mahogany, lignum vitae, tulipwood each have different textures and density. Lignum vita is the most challenging because it is basically very hard and has two shades (beige and brown) inherent in the grain. Working around these gradations provided the inspiration for Tropical Birds, 2001, and *My Mother, Myself, 2007.*

I once acquired some discarded wood from the Steinway Piano workshop (walnut, mahogany). Other pieces come from local trees (tulip, maple) cute down to make room for new houses. While *Tangles Vines, 2003,* was primarily inspired by a collection of poems about mothers and daughters, it was important to me that it was made from a tree felled in my garden.

6. Do specific materials, such as lignum vitae whish has a long history in African sculpture, prompt you to explore styles of figuration found outside Western traditions in art?

Actually, it was African wonderstone that suggested the *Shona* sculpture. I chose to give it a high shine, producing an effect like ebony. It was inspire by the work of the African Shona tribe. In 2002 it won the "Best in Show" award in an Artist Network Exhibition.

7. Does your choice of materials direct you towards certain kinds of images? Or do you decide to explore certain subjects (like queen *Hatshepsut*), and then seek out the kind of stone or wood that would best suit this theme?

I created Hatshepsut after a trip to Egypt. I was so impressed with the Woman/Pharaoh who did so much to improve the lives of her people by maintaining peace and creating beautiful temples. She reigned from 1486-1468 B.C. and managed to rule by relegating her husband and regent to the background. At the same time, yes when I saw the stone I used for this sculpture, it said "Egyptian Head" there was no other way.

8. Auguste Rodin once stated "I choose a block of marble and chop off whatever I don't need." Do you bring the same way of thinking to your studio practice?

Direct carving certainly entails taking material away. But I don't think Rodin was one of my influences.

Finding a form within a block of stone or a piece of wood is an adventure. Materials react differently to the tool. The sounds of stone responding to a chisel is part of the music and rhythm of carving. Wood is more temperamental than stone. It splinters when carved against the grain. Working with lignum vitae is still another experience; it can be so dense and hard that it is used for ships and mallets.

9. Is there room in your studio for "accidents"?

I have incorporated the flaws in some woods, like splits and knots, into the design of *Young Girl* (walnut) and *Tangle Vines* (tulipwood). Onyz cracks easily and one large piece turned into two pieces when it broke in half

(*Polar Birds*, 1996). This is the only piece that sharp, angular lines. I prefer soft, round forms.

10. One of my favorite pieces is the *Reclining Nude, 1989*, made from soapstone. It looks as if you discovered the figure that was already waiting within the stone. Literally a mother from almost at one with the earth, it has remarkable iconic power. Would you consider this a feminist statement?

Unconsciously, yes. For the last thirty years I have been involved with the Women's Movement as a Director of Womanspace, a woman-centered organization. It was informed my work by focusing on the beauty and strengths of womankind.

11. Another favorite is the one title Dancers, 2006. The two figures are wonderfully sensual as their bodies lean into one another, yet neither appears young or classically svelte in the manner of today's modern dancers. Instead, it is as if the Venus of Willendorf had found her perfect mate and they had aged together over many years of loving trust. Would you consider this a portrait of good marriage?

There were inspired by Fernando Botero. I admire his satiric sense of humor very much.

12. Looking at the more abstract pieces, it is easy to recognize your direct homage to Jean Arp, explicitly stated in one of your titles. However, I am also seeing tributes to such artist as Georgia O'Keeffe in the flower forms of such pieces as *Flowerbird, 1991*. Do you ever look at paintings for fresh points of departure?

Sometimes my own garden serves as a palette for my sculpture. But friends and family are very important too. *Fagy, 1990,* a mahogany piece, was completed after my friend Fagy died. It is symbolic of her youthful and naïve approach to life. *Trust* is a tribute to my father; the walnut figures represent the nature of our relationship.

13. One of the newest works in this survey, the male alabaster torso from 2010, is downright sexy. Again, would you consider yourself a feminist in being able to celebrate male strength so forthrightly?

I certainly was not a conscious effort. But now that you mention it, it's very possible. My bachelor's degree in early childhood education from Brooklyn College and a master's degree in Special Education from New York University deepened my connection to women and children, as well as the roles I have lived as a teacher, wife, mother, and daughter.

14. Louise Bourgeois has stated: "I am not what I am, I am what I do with my hands." But of course her work is full of biographical references. Are your images of femininity, motherhood, and timeless archetypes in the end self portraits?

They may not be self portraits, nut they certainly reflect my development, both as a feminist and as a mother. There is a quotation I have always liked by Mark di Suvery: "Your sculpture shall tell who you are."

15. What do you plan to do next?

I'm going continue to sculpt. I have a piece of walnut in progress. Intermittently, I'm writing a memoir and some poetry as well as teaching a memoir-writing class.

PLATES

Allen

Bonding

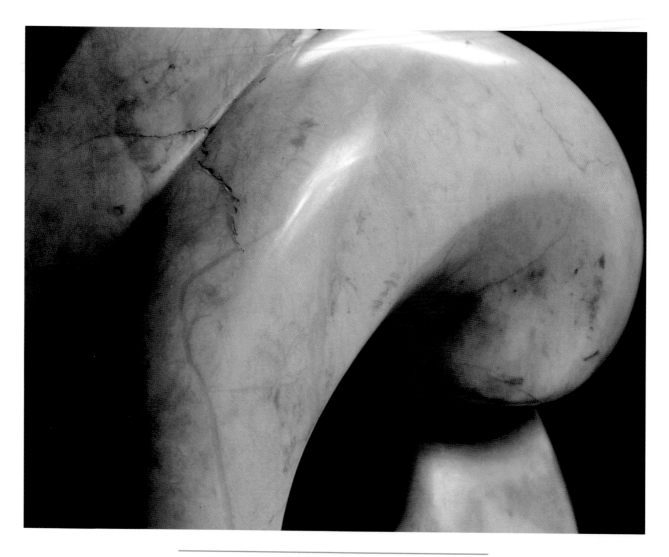

"Caring" [1987]

Two biomorphic figures, carved from alabaster stone, are enfolded with and within one another. This circular configuration of embracing caring figures constitutes an opening into an indeterminate space through which we can "see", imagine a double movement – outward and away in any direction, or back toward a place of greater safety and restorative and reciprocal nurturing: caring.

Darline Levy
ASSOCIATE PROFESSOR OF HISTORY EMERITUS
NEW YORK UNIVERSITY

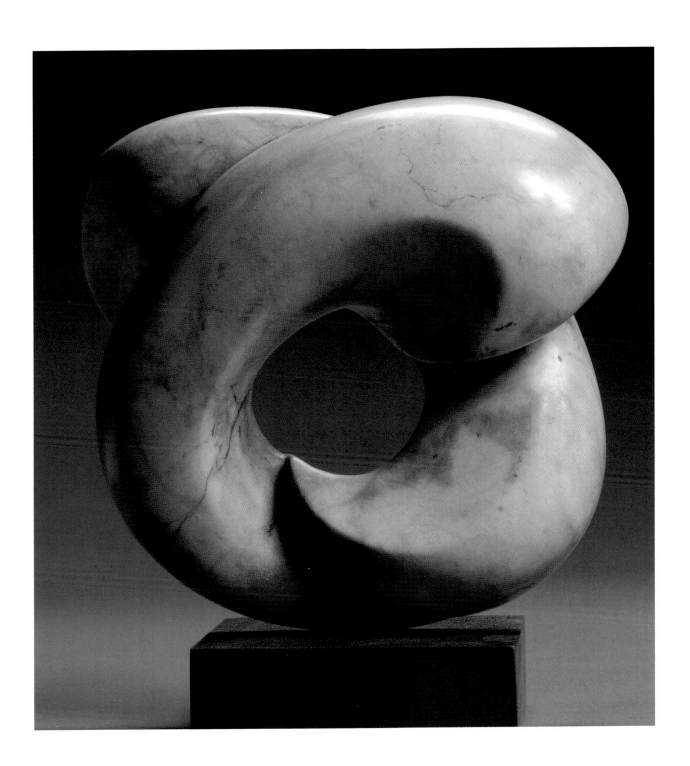

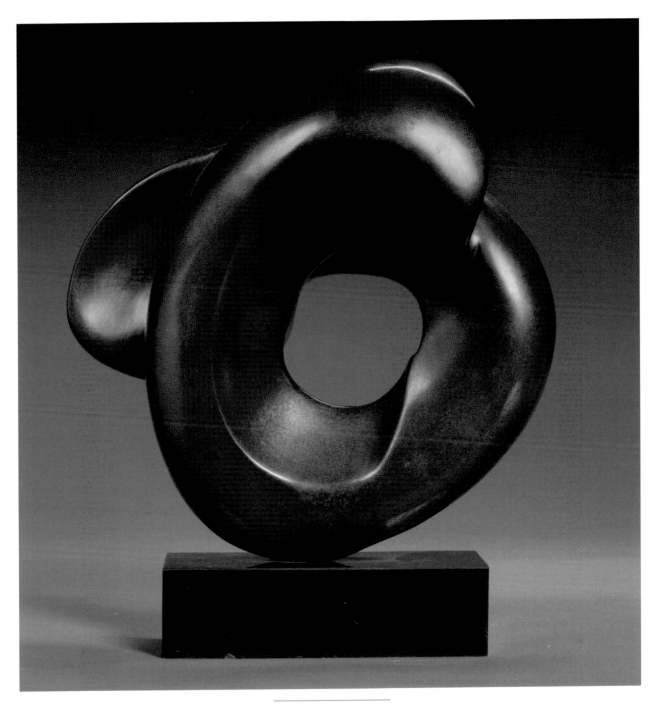

Caring II

Carol

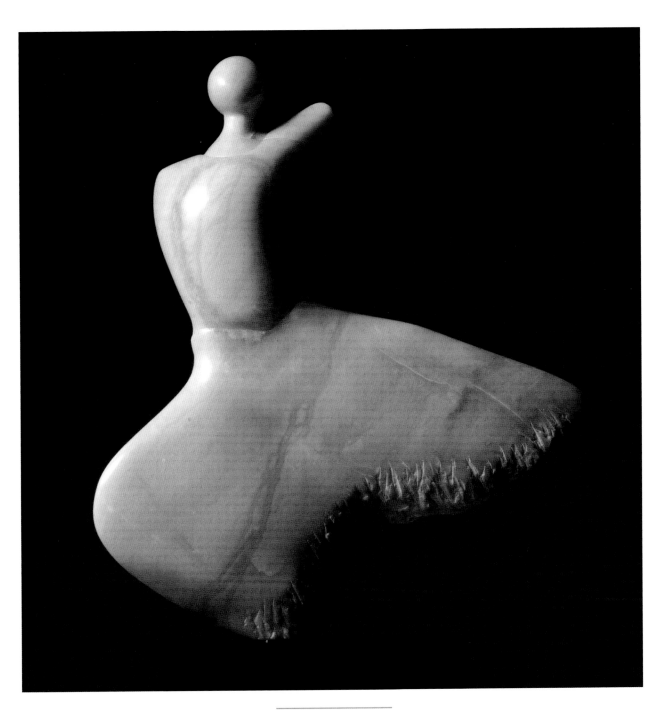

Dancer

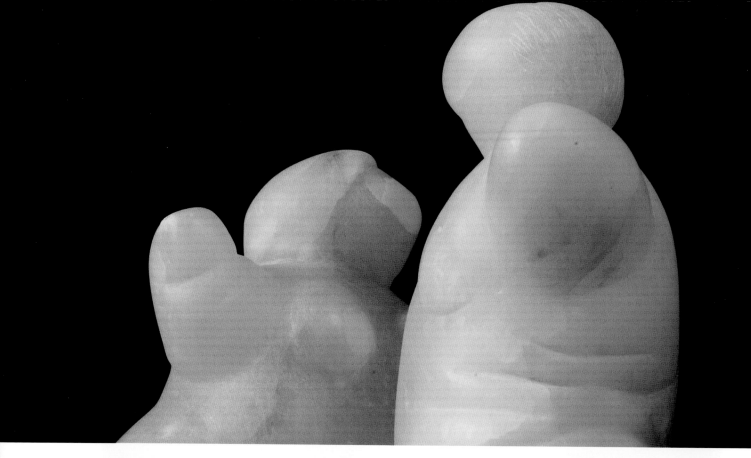

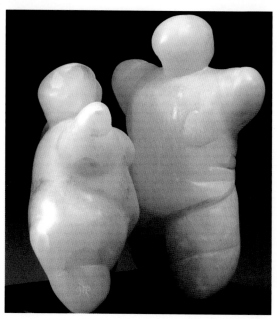

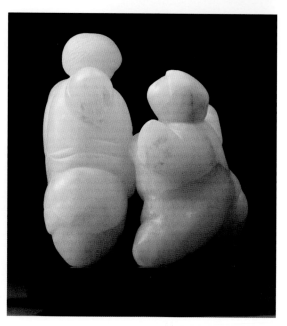

Dancers

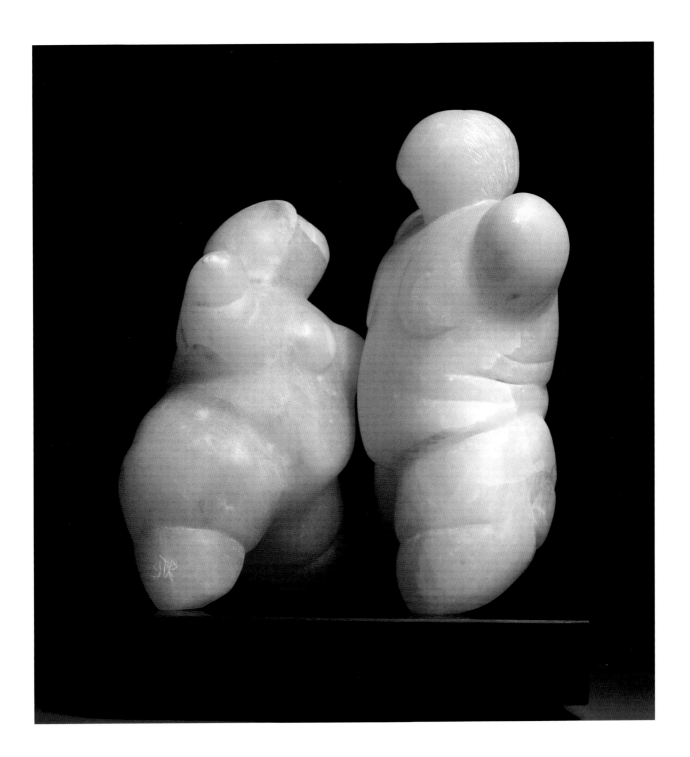

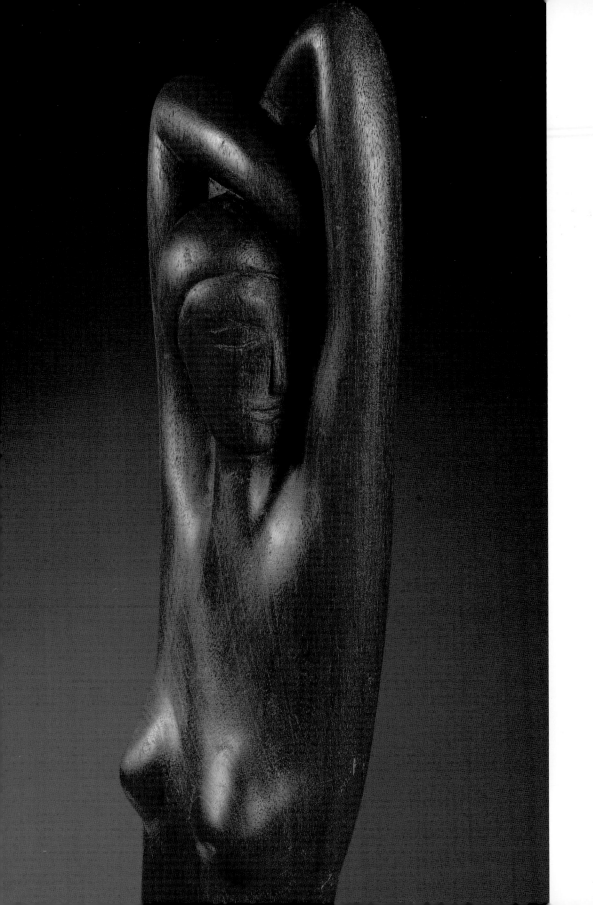

Fagy

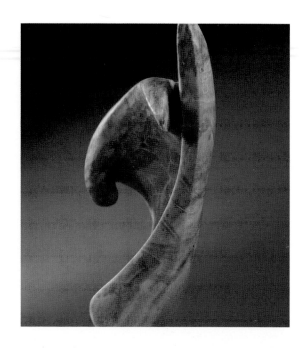

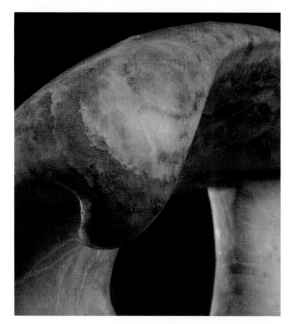

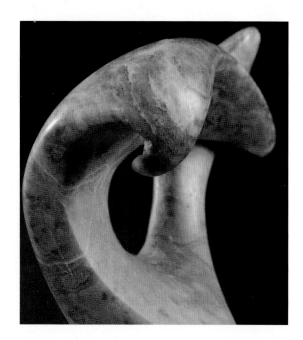

Flight

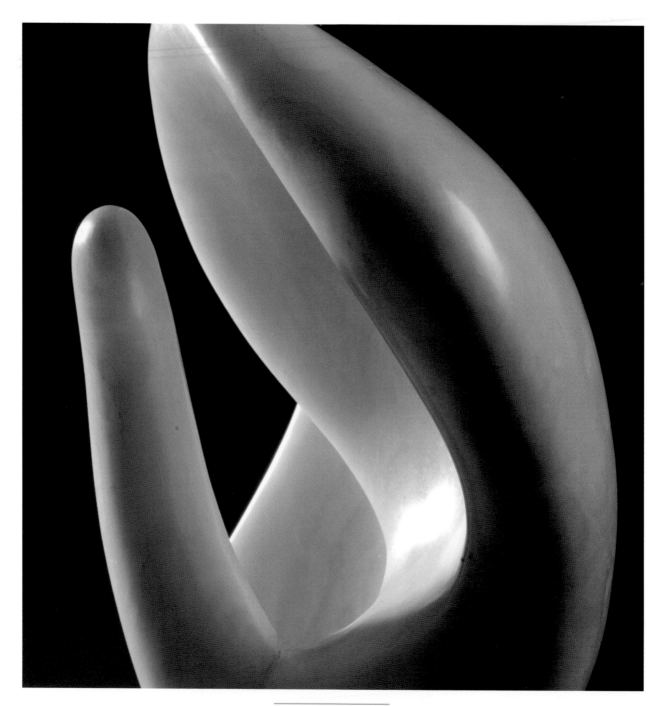

Flowerbird

Free to be me

Hatshepsut

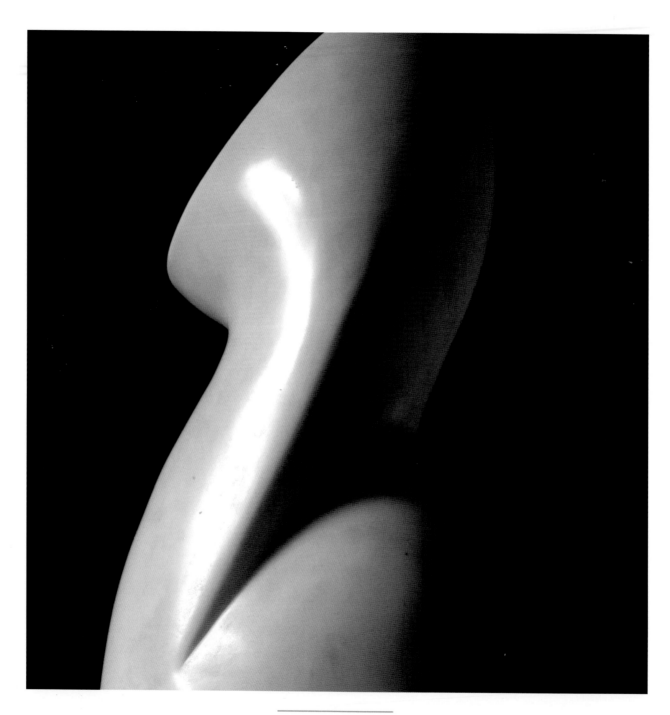

Homage to Arp

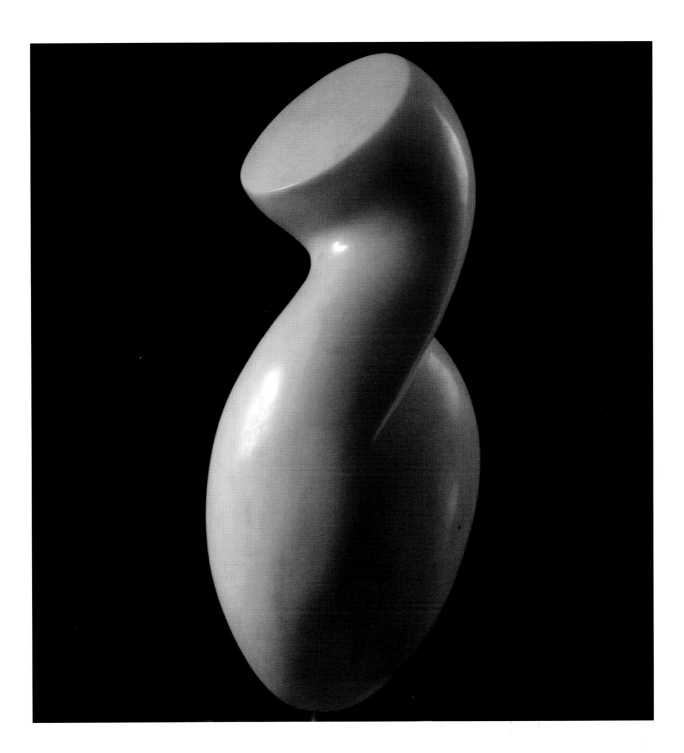

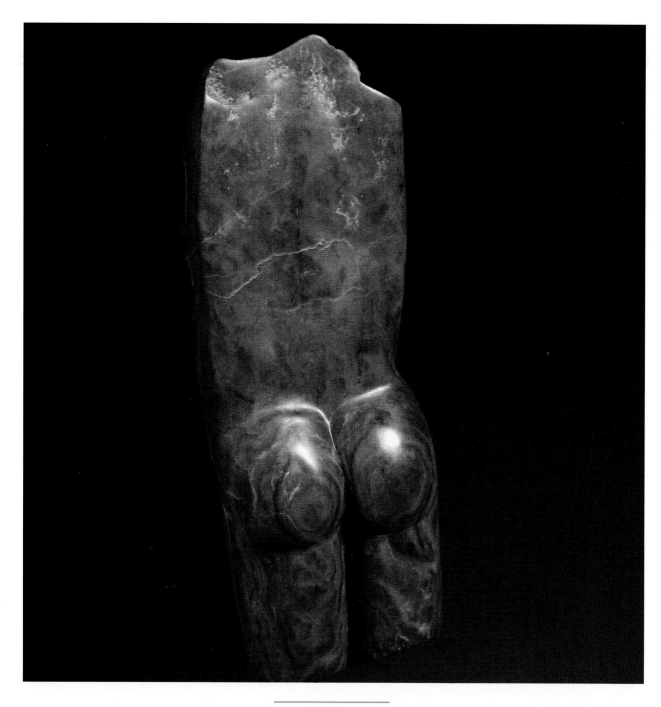

Male Torso

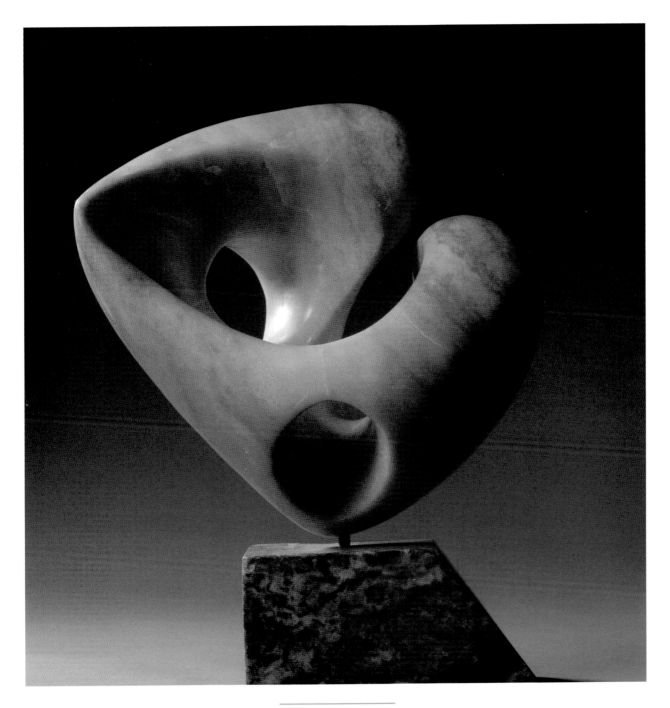

Marriage

"My Mother/Myself" [2007]

Two figures, mother and daughter stand side by side on a common base. Although it is possible to rotate the figure a full 360 degrees, they have been positioned to face not towards but parallel to one another. The mother-daughter pair is sculpted from a block of lignum vitae. The graining and coloring inherent in the wood stamp a patterning on both figures, but differently, bringing into relief and heightening their connection/separation. Roth configures "My Mother/Myself" as a pair standing apart yet together, two separate individuals, profoundly connected in a relational tie that binds and holds.

Darline Levy
Associate Professor of History Emeritus
New York University

"Mother and Child" [2000]

In this sculpture, carved out of a single block of grey soapstone, a hieratic mother figure holds her child against her body; the child's head rests against the mother's right shoulder; its embracing arms reaches across her chest to grasp her left shoulder. This configuration awakens and engages a deep and abiding human need, a longing to recover and re-engage with the experience of holding on and being held in a relationship of unconditional nurturing love.

Darline Levy
ASSOCIATE PROFESSOR OF HISTORY EMERITUS
NEW YORK UNIVERSITY

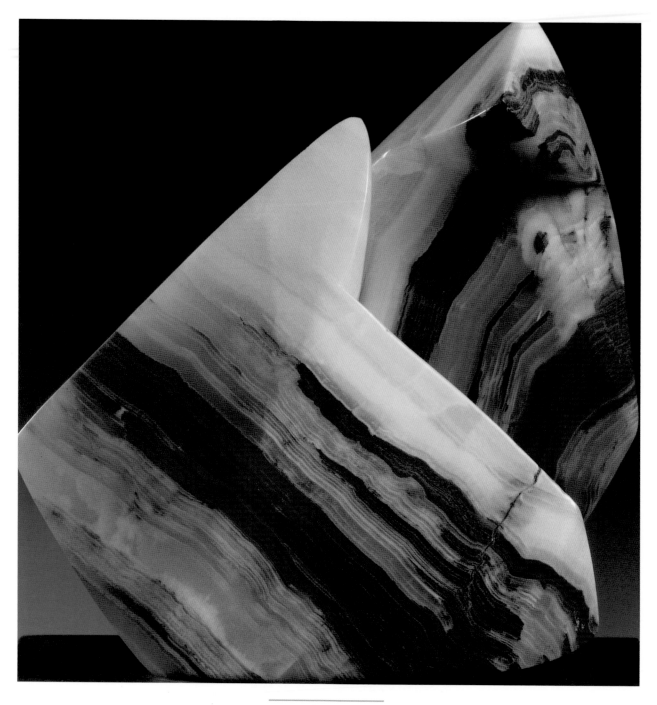

Polar Birds

Pregnant Woman

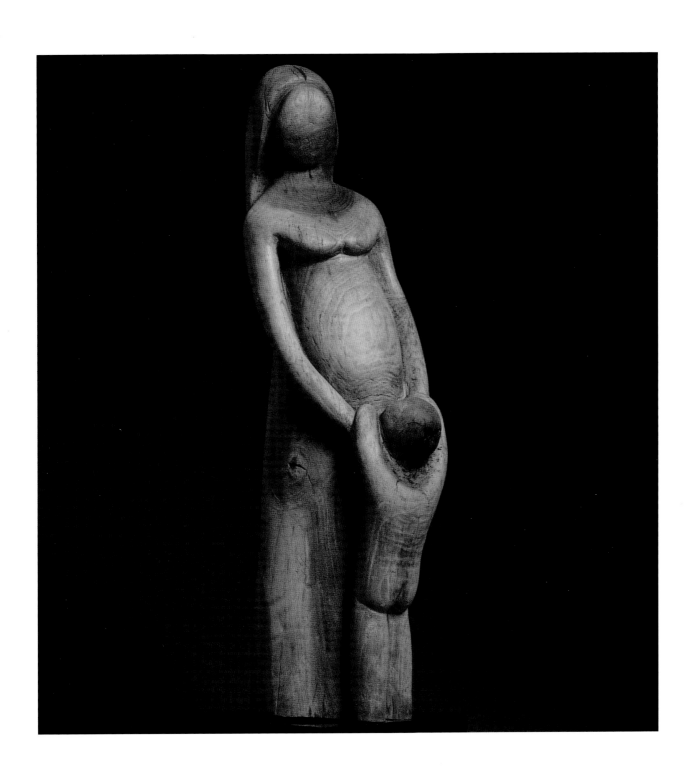

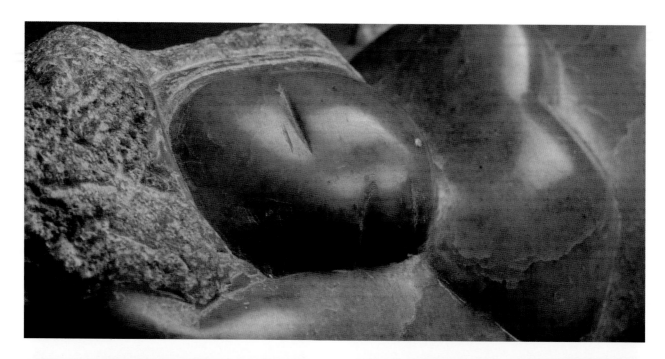

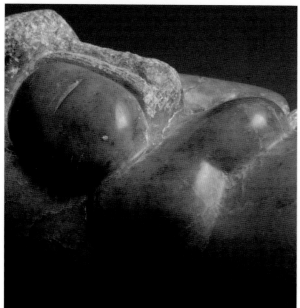

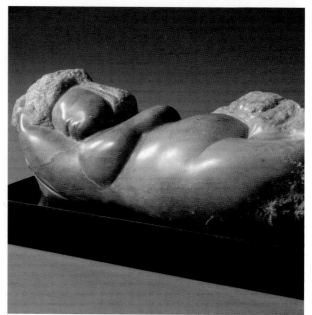

Reclining Nude

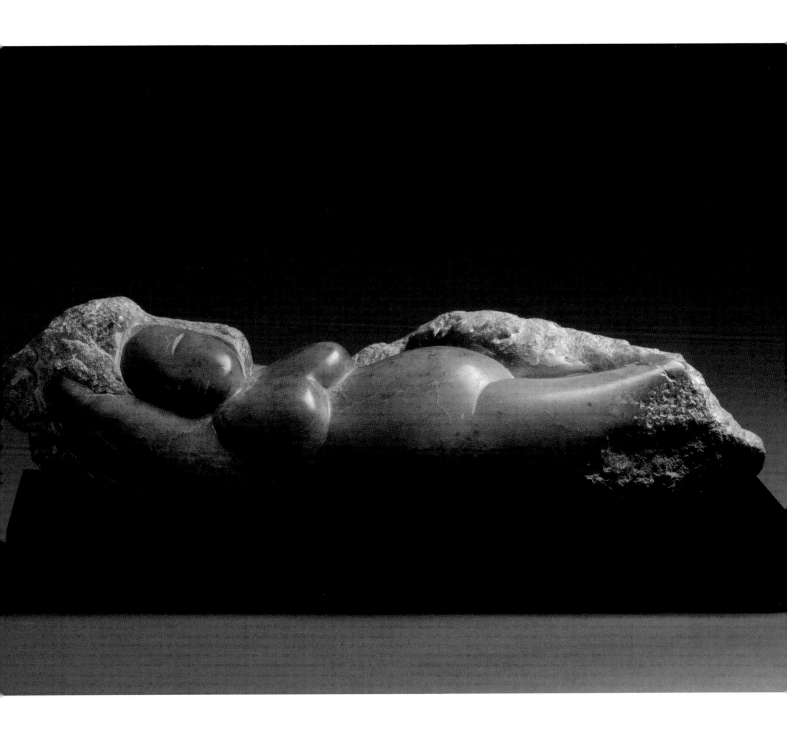

Serenity

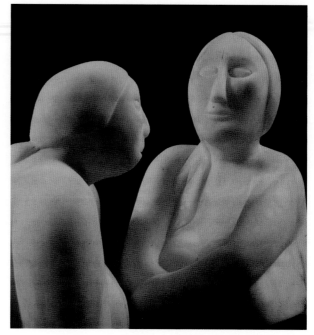

"Sharing Wisdom" [2004]

The busts of two women – elderly in appearance, weighty in mass and with archaizing features -- have been sculpted from a block of white veined alabaster – a stone with exceptional quality of appearing to absorb and emanate light. The busts are mounted on a single base and positioned to face one another, as though in conversation. The figure on the left, with head inclined and in an attitude of concentrated attentiveness, leans in toward the figure on the right whose upright posture and stance – shoulders drawn back arms folded across the chest – evoke a imposing presence. The sculptor's title names and completes the connection that brings and holds them together: Sharing Wisdom, a signifier for valuing, sharing, preserving the store of accumulated knowledge and experience.

Darline Levy
ASSOCIATE PROFESSOR OF HISTORY
NEW YORK UNIVERSITY

Shona

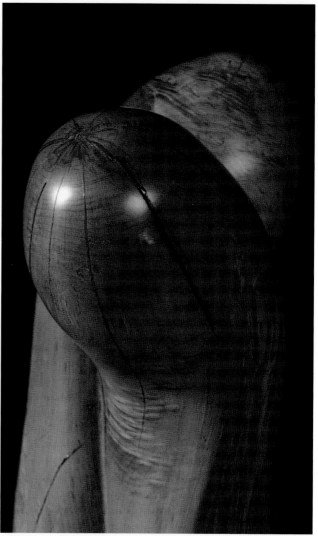

Tangled Vines

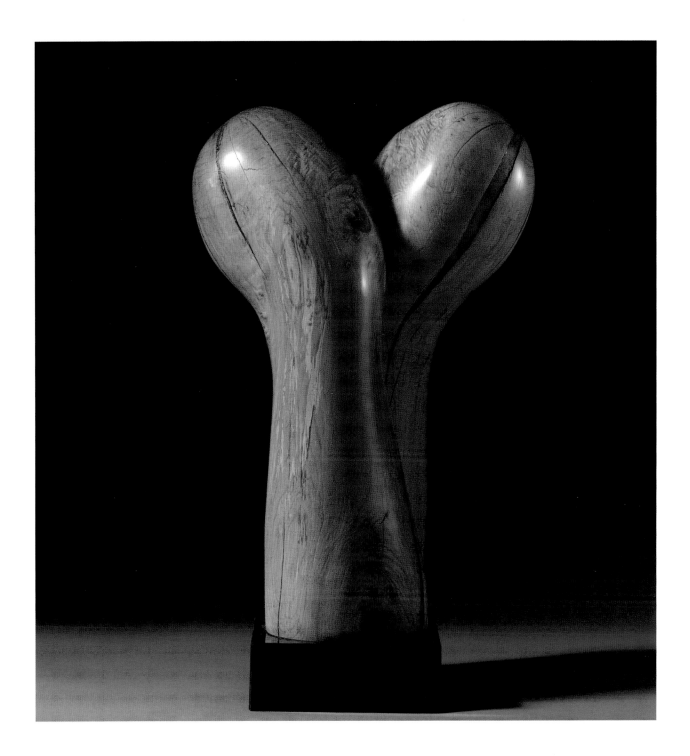

The Spirits Move Me

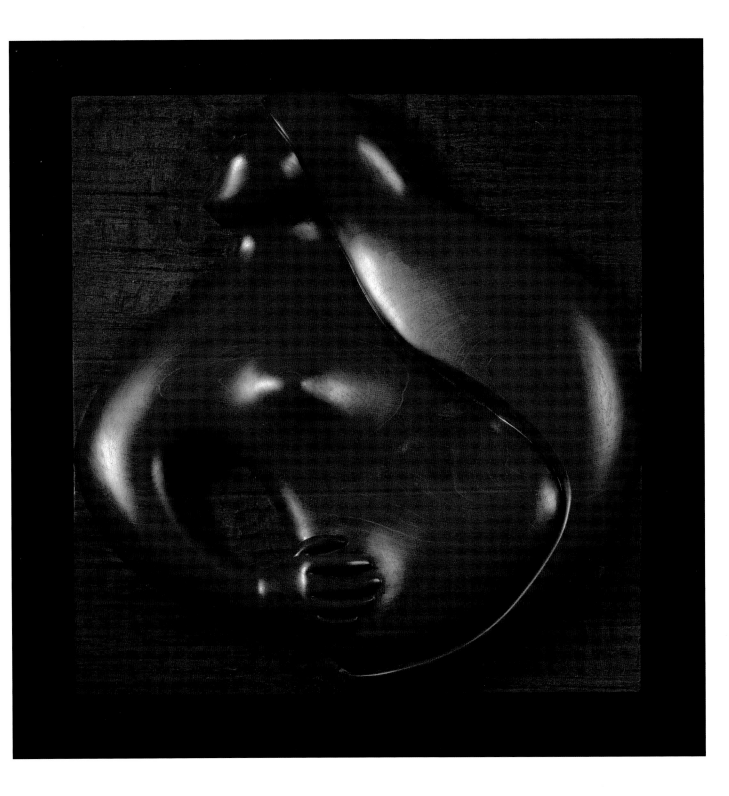

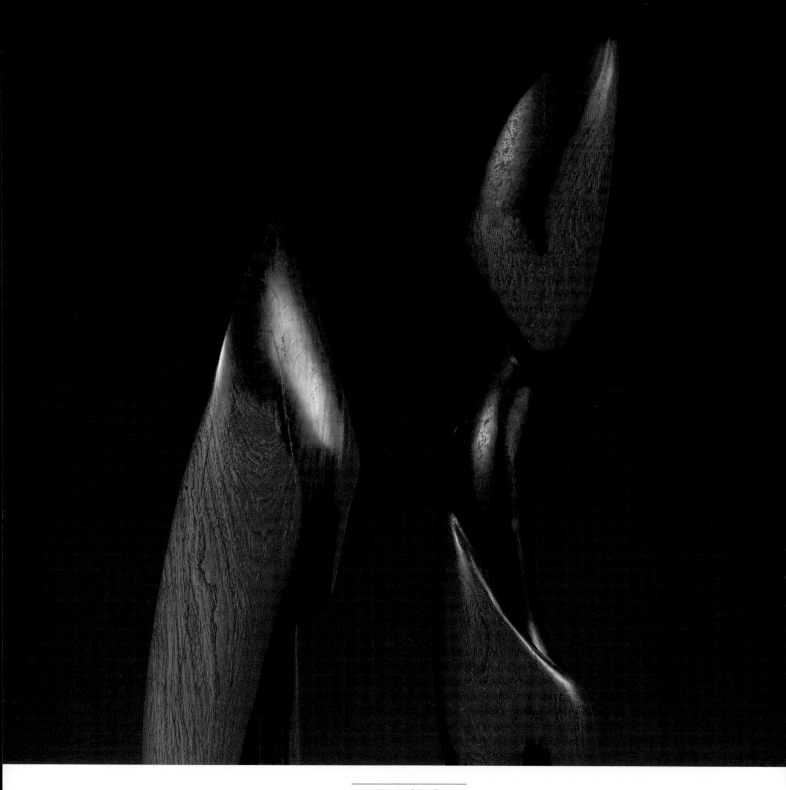

Tropical Birds

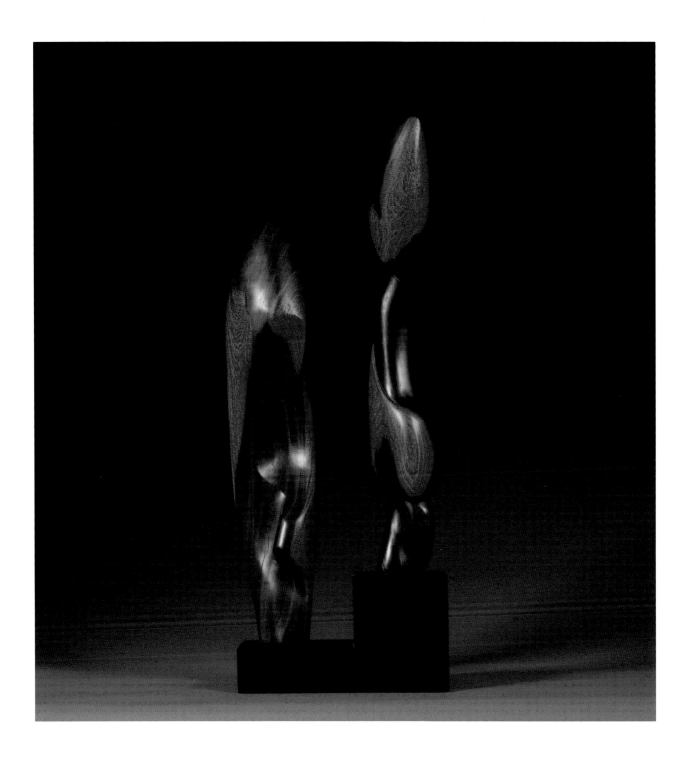

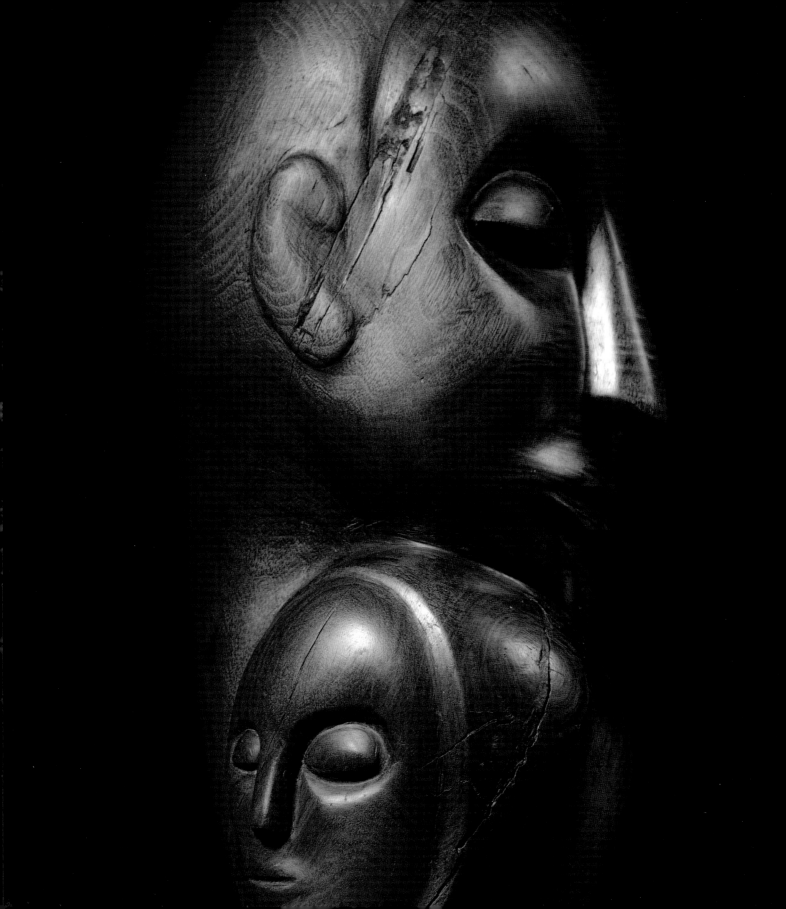

Trust

Unfurled

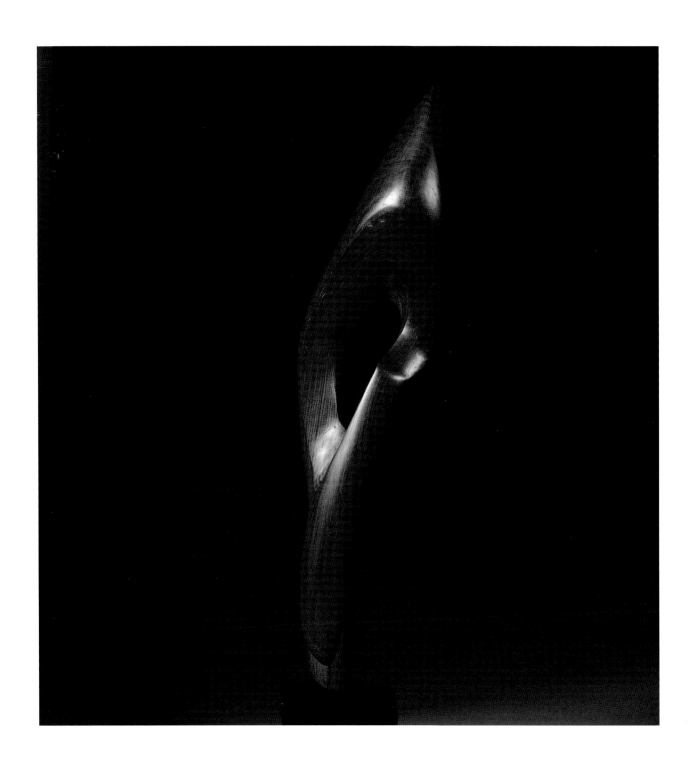

Love

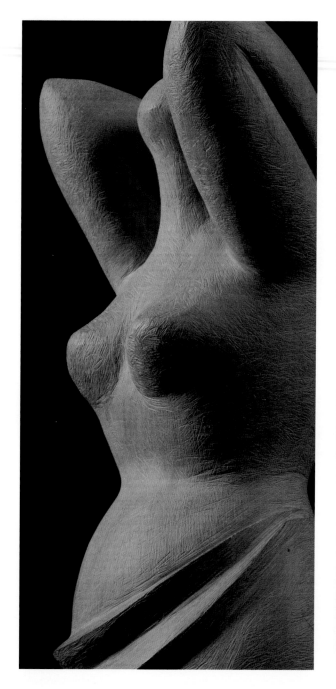

Woman

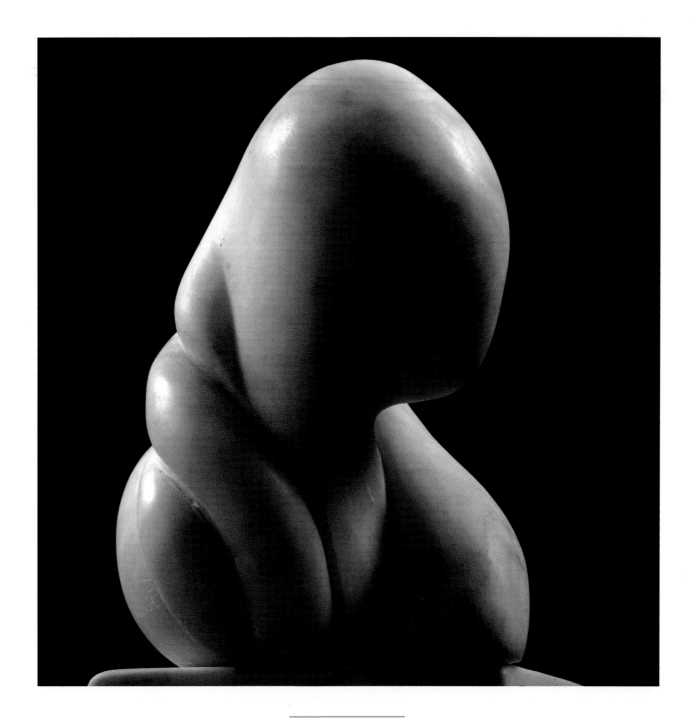

Woman with Hair

Woman's back

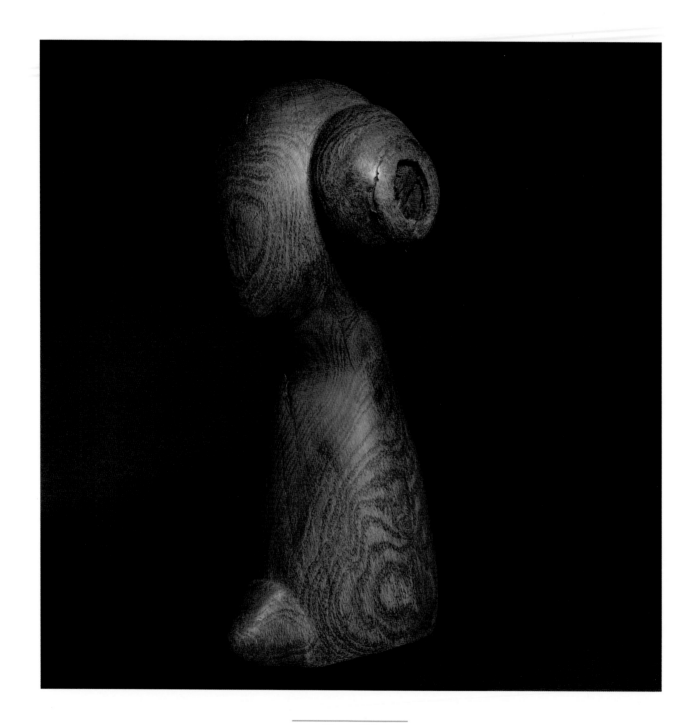

Young Girl

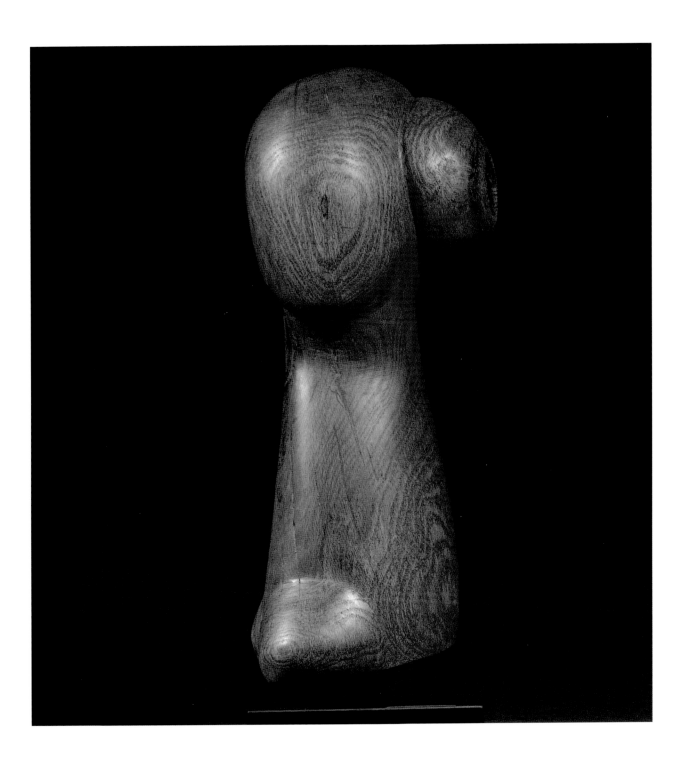

Down to Earth

A Shy Woman

Works Chronology

Page	Title	Material	Dimensions	Year
31	**Carol**	Clay (fired)	12"x11"x6"	1985
23	**Allen**	Clay (fired)	12"x11"x6"	1985
83	**Woman with Hair**	Alabaster	13"x6"x5"	1986
27	**Caring**	Alabaster	12"x11"x6"	1987
29	**Caring II**	Bronze	25"x8"x6"	1987
77	**Unfurled**	Coco-bola wood	17"x7"x6"	1988
61	**Reclinig Nude**	Soapstone	13"x12"x81/2"	1989
25	**Bonding**	Grey alabaster	13"x13"x81/2"	1990
37	**Fagy**	Honduras mahogany	43"x6"x31/2"	1990
41	**Flowerbird**	White alabaster	21"x7"x10"	1991
43	**Free To Be Me**	Walnut	43"x7"x6"	1992
89	**Down to Earth**	Limestone	53"x12"x111/2	1992
47	**Homage to Arp**	Marble	21"x6"x8"	1993
59	**Pregnant Woman**	Walnut	29"x9"x8"	1994
45	**Hatshepsut**	Alabaster	17"x13"x8"	1995
57	**Polar Birds**	Onyx	11"x101/2"x7"	1996
75	**Trust**	Walnut	27"x6"x6"	1997
51	**Marriage**	Alabaster	16"x11"x7"	1998
81	**Woman**	African Wonderstone	22"x9"x73/4"	1999
63	**Serenity**	Brown alabaster	17"x12"x9"	2000
54	**Mother and Child**	Soapstone	17"x5"x31/2"	2000
39	**Flight**	Alabaster	14"x9"x11"	2001
73	**Tropical Birds**	Lignum vitae	24"x10"x6"	2001
87	**Young Girl**	Walnut	21"x9"x51/2"	2002
67	**Shona**	African Wonderstone	21"x8"x71/2"	2002
69	**Tangled Vines**	Tulipwood	21"x8"x71/2"	2002
71	**The Spirit Moves Me**	Honduras mahogony	21"x21"x4"	2003
78	**Love**	Alabaster	13"x6"x5"	2003
65	**Sharing Wisdom**	Alabaster	14"x16"x10"	2004
85	**Woman's Back**	Alabaster	20"x13"x6"	2005
85	**Dancers**	Alabaster	11"x10"x7'	2006
53	**My Mother/ Myself**	Lignum vitae	23"x11"x71/2"	2007
33	**Dancer**	Alabaster	19"x11"x4"	2008
91	**Shy Woman**	Limestone	25"x9"x7"	2009
49	**Male Torso**	Variegated alabaster	25"x8"x6"	2010

Acknowledgments

I was inspired to incorporate the images of my sculptures into a book and subsequently into a show by fellow writers and artists, as well as family members among who was Darline Levy, who saw beyond what the sculpture seemed to say and whose enthusiasm gave me the courage to pursue this project. Alison de Lima Greene for contributed her professional experience.

I began with Pauline Shapiro, a young, talented photographer who took the photographs, showing great sensitivity to the work. I credit her patience in photographing many views of each piece showing them to their best advantage.

Phyllis Brusiloff, who has been an admirer of my work, convinced me represent her work to the QCC Art Gallery. With her encouragement, the editing of this project went forward.

My daughter, Lisa, has been involved in this venture from the beginning. She referred me to Pauline Shapiro, who is her colleague, and provided graphics and emails when necessary. My daughter Jan filled in with computer know-how in consultation with Lisa. My thanks also go to Matthew Hauptman, my grandson, for typing up my hand written notes. My husband Marty inspired the title of the work, "A Journey in Stone and Wood" and gave me the support and encouragement to proceed.

To all of them I give my hearty thanks.